EXERCISE DESIGN FOR THE JOINT FORCE 2020 BRIGADE COMBAT TEAM

> In the 21st century, we do not have the luxury of deciding which challenges to prepare for and which to ignore. We must overcome the full spectrum of threats—the conventional and the unconventional; the nation-state and the terrorist network; the spread of deadly technologies and the spread of hateful ideologies; 18th century-style piracy and 21st century cyber tactics.[1]

> —President Barack Obama, 2009

The maneuver Combat Training Centers (CTCs)[2] have evolved to generate an unprecedented level of realism and intensity to guarantee that the Soldiers, sailors, airmen, Marines, civilians, and partners training there before deploying to the current fights are ready for the situations they are about to confront.[3] As the Army comes out of Afghanistan and Iraq and adjusts to the strategic environment of 2020 for its next decades of operations, the CTCs must sustain their tradition of excellence and also be agile to remain the premier venues for force preparation.

Recent U.S. experience in Afghanistan and Iraq has shown that the first 100 days of a unit's commitment in combat is its most dangerous; all advantages the Army can provide Soldiers to be able to assimilate more rapidly to the environment, social dynamics, and opposition tactics during this initial period when the enemy is testing them should save lives and enhance unit effectiveness—advancing intended national outcomes.[4] The U.S. Army's capstone CTC training event exercise design[5] and the associated scenarios should be continuously adapted to remain relevant for expected real-world operations, realistic in the portrayal of societal dynamics, and challenging for participants at every echelon.[6]

Complex challenges, even those beyond a unit's present level of proficiency, will push them to learn, grow and improve. As such, CTC exercise design, with the battle space texture and atmospherics[7] generated for BCT rotations must foster the conditions that ensure our units develop the high-end collective proficiency across a broad range of possible challenges in order to give them dominance in complex environments against adversaries possessing the home-team advantage.[8] As the Army prepares its units to employ Full Spectrum Operations (FSO) competencies across the range of conflicts; readiness for unified operations on land restores the nation's decision-makers a critical-degree of flexibility under any scenario.[9] Sustaining the utmost fidelity within the CTC Contemporary Operational Environment (COE)[10] will assist the Army's leadership in setting the conditions that allow our units to have the most realistic and challenging training experiences short of combat.

Well-trained and well-led ground forces at the tactical level are essential in generating the strategic effects that "prevent" adversaries from escalating conflicts, "shape" the international environment, and where challenged, "win" decisively and dominantly.[11] This paper advances ideas on adjustments at the Army's maneuver CTCs, specifically the National Training Center (NTC) at Fort Irwin, California, to optimally improve BCT readiness for undertaking missions that span the spectrum of conflict. As the NTC has capably generated comprehensive preparation for recent and present operations, it must transform to portray future ground force challenges; all these tasks should be practiced against a variety of simulated threats in a training environment first.[12] NTC's operational design must enhance readiness by building upon unit proficiency in core areas: mastering their weapon systems, fluidly transitioning between the skills required for different missions, and practicing working with other Army enablers and the Joint, Interagency, Intergovernmental, and Multinational (JIIM) community.

The first section of this paper traces the NTC's evolution from the 1980s to the present as a basis for evaluating prudent additional adjustments should be incorporated for future rotations that will sustain collective training experiences with cutting-edge relevancy to the force. The second section reviews current analysis and projections concerning the global strategic environment through 2020, to include allies, friends, and adversaries. What roles does the strategic environment suggest for U.S. landpower? How should the Army organize to provide joint force commanders "the ability to deter conflict, prevail in war, and succeed in a wide range of contingencies?"[13] The last section culminates with recommending specific adjustments to NTC's COE. The main recommendations target three of the COE's "operational variables";[14] adjustments focusing on the depiction of the "infrastructure, social, and economic variables." Accounting for fiscal and other resource constrained realities, this study finishes with ideas on how to incrementally implement these ideas, emphasizing "smarter" stewardship over increasingly scarce resources. If implemented, these adjustments will aid NTC in its quest to heighten unit readiness. In doing so, NTC will be on azimuth with what General Martin Dempsey seeks with his comments indicating that we must "make the scrimmage as hard as the game."[15]

Evolution of the NTCs (1980s to Present)

As part of the U.S. Army's post-Vietnam efforts to build and train a highly professional all-volunteer force, senior leaders recognized they faced a capabilities gap for exercising large-scale combined arms and maneuver in training that would produce unit proficiency to assure dominance over existing or potential adversaries. In 1979, the

3

Army designated Fort Irwin, California to serve as the home of its initial maneuver CTC. The first maneuver brigade task force rotation was executed in 1982. The high-end multi-echelon training solution that evolved over the next decade included a combination of live-fire exercises and force-on-force high-intensity Major Combat Operations (MCO) against a professional opposing force (OPFOR) that employed conventional adversary doctrine and tactics; all conducted in a battle space of sufficient size and complexity to portray the brigade's fight. Unlike any home-station live-training events, the CTC rotations provided exclusive opportunities that allowed commanders to exercise everything and all systems against a backdrop that included applicable stressors. By the 1990s, in the absence of actual routine large-scale combat commitments, maneuver brigades trained in earnest for possible real-world commitments, but short of real wars, units considered CTC rotations to be the "Super Bowl"—their nearly annual opportunity to test their metal against a worthy adversary.[16]

To generate assured training outcomes, the NTC established the NTC Operations Group (OPSGROUP) to perform roles covering exercise design, scenario development, while fulfilling all operational and tactical-level higher and adjacent headquarters interaction with the Rotational Training Unit (RTU). However, OPSGROUP's most visible mission is performed by Observer/Controllers (O/Cs) that shadow the RTU, at every echelon, providing in-depth feedback through a doctrinal lens. O/C feedback provided the Army-level as well as RTU leaders highly valued external assessments of where improvements were needed recommendations towards where they could afford to shift priorities and otherwise adjust fire.

A heavy conventional brigade was also based Fort Irwin, a role that the 11th Armored Cavalry Regiment (11th ACR) has performed since 1994, and charged with working with OPSGROUP and providing a near peer combined arms adversary that employed home terrain advantage to more than challenge the best U.S. Army brigades. The NTC's training area, which became known as the "maneuver box" or simply as the "box," is the world's only instrumented training adequate for heavy brigade-sized formations executing both life fire and force-on-force training.[17] NTC's box comprises some of the continental U.S's most inhospitable terrain: a wide expanse of the high Mojave Desert, complete with mountains, wadis, bowls, and generally restrictive mobility corridors.

In the 1990s, compounded realities of recent operations including Operation Just Cause in Panama, Somalia, Haiti, and the increasing number of U.S. commitments to Stability Operations in the Balkans influenced the Army's and CTC emphasis on providing adequate training conditions for units to operate in battlefield dynamics that included the necessity to interact with population in order to accomplish the civil aspects necessary to achieve operational objectives. Although each CTC rotation included offensive, defensive, and stability operations tasks associated with FSO, NTC's COE primarily pitted the RTU against a more traditional, heavy mechanized adversary—NTC did not make the same-degree of transition to replicating irregular warfare (IW) and stability operations as did its sister CTCs. The experience and template of the exercise design used at the other CTCs during the 1990s, during their versions of FSO and Mission Rehearsal Exercises (MREs) for specific operations,[18] did however greatly influence the skeleton used by all CTCs to train the force for commitments in Afghanistan and Iraq since 2003.

In 2003 the Army and Marine Corps adjusted their CTC rotational scenarios from a FSO focus that prepared units for all manner of contingencies to MREs construct that was limited to those units already designated to deploy to Afghanistan or Iraq.[19] Each Service directed specific pre-deployment training requirements, many incorporated within a unit's MRE, prior to certifying readiness for overseas employment.[20] NTC captured the essence of its new mandate as providing "tough, realistic, joint and combined arms training in interagency, and intergovernmental and multinational venues across the spectrum of conflict in order to prepare BCTs and other units for combat."[21]

Unlike previous traditional NTC rotations that exercised a range of warfare competencies, the first major adjustment is that NTC MRE rotations place the RTU under an Irregular Warfare COIN environment for the duration of their 14 training days in the box. The relentless demands to provide trained and ready units for both theaters required the NTC to operate at its full throughput capacity, eleven rotations per year, with an average of 6,228[22] service members participating as members of the RTU during each rotation.

The second significant adjustment was altering NTC's exercise design to compensate for the shortfall in extensive home-station unit training caused by high-demand for deployable units, short dwell time, and late personnel fill. Having unit's arrive at NTC with a lower-level of collective proficiency required time-phased modifications in training focus that begin before units enter the box. NTC cadre works with the RTU to focus on individual and squad-level proficiency as well as concentrating on mission-specific equipment proficiency. Cadre and contractors provide individual and small group training sessions or over the shoulder assistance that provide a quick infusion of the latest enemy tactics, appropriate Tactics, Techniques, and Procedures (TTPs), and technical assistance for a variety of systems.[23]

The next MRE adjustment targeted rapidly building collective proficiency and integration at the platoon, company, and staff-levels by employing a combination of Situational Training Exercise (STX) lanes, live-fires, and staff Command Post Exercises (CPXs) during the first seven days the RTU is in the box, all reflecting operations required in the current fight. To carve-out time dedicated to work these other focus areas, NTC reduced the force-on-force phase of the rotation from the entire fourteen days in the box to the last six or seven days. Throughout the rotation, the RTU receives in-depth analysis, coaching, and targeted training assistance from the O/Cs to minimize the number of deadly mistakes and first time experiences the RTU experiences in theater.[24] The combat effectiveness of BCTs and other units that have completed CTC rotations since the Army implemented its post-2003 construct validate the value of this training. Preparing these units in the ever increasingly complex and realistic NTC box have also required the NTC, its supporting, and partner organizations to take the Army's premier live collective training experience up a notch, far beyond the degree of JIIM integration previously attempted.

The adjustments that have produced the changes in the tailored complexity, environmental realism, cultural dynamics, and tempo over what was portrayed a decade ago are profound. For example, General Dempsey noted that during his 1997 NTC rotation as the 3rd Armored Cavalry Regiment's Commander, OPSGROUP incorporated five data sources to generate 2,500 information-and-intelligence injects that drove the tactical scenario. In contrast, also covering 14 training days, to produce a BCT MRE in 2009, OPSGROUP employed 27 data sources and generating approximately 1.2 million information-and-intelligence injects that are all prepared and scripted in advance to fuel the complexity required for the COE.[25] OPSGROUP weaves scripts for each rotation are several hundred pages long, incorporating 112 major events.[26]

They define roles and layout hundreds of threads that are interwoven and fed into play to push the RTU to address, and resolve or mitigate root causes of instability, which can include: culture, politics, foreign influences, economics, social conditions, and religious sectarian behaviors.[27] Scenario evolution is not lockstep; instead it is more "controlled free-play" accommodating RTU reaction to events and adjusting accordingly along lines of branches and sequels.[28] Exercise design for MRE rotations is predominantly weighted on focusing units on defeating the insurgency and stabilizing the operating environment through shaping activities that integrate all JIIM capabilities. O/Cs and other institutional enablers collaborate to ensure the RTU is infused with the most recent lessons learned, trained on new systems and processes, and following over-the-shoulder coaching, are prepared to succeed in actual combat.

Previously focused more on the nation's traditional heavy, mechanized threat, NTC needed more adjustments than the other CTCs to transform its physical environment to replicate a COIN mandate. Fortunately, the wartime requirements came with a torrent of previously rare funding that allowed the rapid conversion of the NTC box, a land area about the size of the state of Rhode Island (839 square miles),[29] from possessing practically no buildings to replicating an Afghan or Iraqi province. By 2004,

NTC's limited urban portrayal still required units to use a great deal of imagination to consider small clusters of metal MILVAN shipping containers and some pre-fabricated wooden sheds at several tank trail intersections to be villages.[30]

Contracted firms, some that assist with Hollywood movie set design and associated pyrotechnics effects, methodically converted the Box's vast desert expanses into a battle space that although not the mirror-image of either Afghanistan or Iraq was close in most respects. By 2008, the Box was covered with a bustling array of over a thousand habitable and fairly authentic buildings constituting thirteen towns and villages.[31] As a major portion of one of the major towns, NTC teamed with the Defense Advanced Research Projects Agency (DARPA) and jointly built the state-of-the-art National Urban Warfare Complex.[32] To further reflect the environment units would face on deployment, cave and tunnel complexes were added in some locations in addition to some walled compounds so that units could practice needed TTPs. NTC also added seven Forward Operating Bases (FOBs) and numerous Joint Security Sites (JSS), and Combat Outposts (COPs) to accurately depict the settings where units would live, operate, and fostered the conditions necessary force protection measures.[33]

Equal if not exceeding the changes to the physical environment, the changes to how NTC replicates the human terrain is revolutionary compared to when the battle space only contained the RTU, the conventional OPFOR, and the O/Cs. By 2009, OPFOR Soldiers augmented by contractors portrayed the HN security forces (army, police, and sometimes border guards), government, other allied forces, the population, representatives from various international or humanitarian relief organizations, the media, and several insurgent networks. Depending on whether a given rotation was representative of Afghanistan or Iraq, separate immigrant natives of that country served in the major language and culturally specific roles. Fielding a composite force of 2,200 personnel (1,500 Soldiers and 700 civilian contractors) daily, the 11th ACR brought the COE to life with all its complexity.[34] All role players are trained in the target cultural dynamics, provided representative dress, and receive specific identities, background information, occupations, and responsibilities that guide their actions.[35] Those performing civilian roles use a government owned fleet of civilian cars, trucks, and busses to transit the Box and undertake their various responsibilities.

NTC efforts to pull-in all forms of relevant help from across the JIIM community are undertaken in response to lessons learned in Afghanistan, Iraq, and other recent operations. NTC has succeeded in producing an ever expanding array of rotational participants and supporting enabler organizations. Every rotation includes at least one company, or larger, SOF element from one of the Services. Besides also providing the SOF component opportunity to exercise within this premier training environment, CTC participation in battle space "owned by conventional brigade has fostered much closer coordination, and even mutual support, as our conventional and unconventional forces prosecute their separate mission mandates. In addition to the Air Force elements that are organic attachments to the maneuver BCTs, the U.S. Air Force operates Green Flag-West providing air-land battle coverage. Permanent part Air Force elements work with Nellis Air Force Base, Nevada to synchronize the both fixed-wing and UAV providing both close air support and ISR coverage to the RTU by joint service and coalition assets. Resident offices at Fort Irwin for both the Joint Fires Interoperability

Integration Team (JFIIT) and Joint IED Defeat Organization (JIEDDO) adds synergistic effects to quickly incorporating new threat tactics and infusing lessons learned.[36]

Routine NTC collaboration with various other DOD and interagency partners contributes to the incremental scenario enrichment, up-to-the minute currency, and reach-back assistance. Several other government agencies, including the Bureau of Alcohol, Tobacco, Firearms and Explosives (ATF), the Central Intelligence Agency (CIA), the Federal Bureau of Investigation (FBI), and Department of State (DOS), have their employees regularly imbedded within the RTU's staff to enhance training value for all parties. Law Enforcement Professionals (LEPs), Human Terrain Teams, Cultural Advisors, and numerous translator/interpreters round-out the routine infusion of specialized enablers that are attached to the RTU for a typical rotation.[37]

Although the senior Army leadership wanted to return CTC rotations to more broadly exercise FSO competencies for at least select units years ago, the realities of CTC maximum throughput capacity unrelenting demand to prepare maneuver BCTs for deployment delayed first iteration of a FSO CTC rotation until October 2010. That proof-of-principle FSO rotation against a hybrid threat was executed at JRTC was followed by one at JMRC in October 2011.[38] The NTC held a FSO rotation in March 2012, the first in over ten years that was not exclusively focused on the counterinsurgency fight.[39]

The Strategic Security Environment (Present to Joint Force 2020)

In many ways, the collapse of the Iron Curtain in 1989 signaled the world's entry into an increasingly complex and uncertain future. Political, economic, informational, and cultural ties are interconnected.[40] The days of unchallenged American hegemony are over; the future suggests that, in many ways, we will live in an increasingly multi-polar world. Certain states will seize increasing roles as "regional powers," each having differing expectations towards their privileges within their spheres of influence, thus triggering heightened tensions. Trends that include changing demographics, exponential population growth within underdeveloped regions, and unsustainable services in rising megacities have fostered conditions where the underprivileged and disenfranchised are demanding change. The additional effects of shifting economic patterns, nearly immediate access to global news and communications, religiously oriented extremism, climate change, fuel, food and water scarcity, natural disasters, and pandemics portray the dynamics our decision makers must include within their calculus.[41]

With these factors in mind, in his February 2012 testimony before congress, General Dempsey stressed that the difference between the current drawdown from those after Vietnam and the Cold War is that they were done as the U.S. entered "a period of relative stability." The challenges confronting the U.S. now are vastly different. He stated, "to my personal military judgment formed over 38 years, we are living in the most dangerous time in my lifetime."[42]

After a decade of war, the dawn of 2012 finds the U.S. military finally out of Iraq, Osama bin Laden eliminated, and security responsibilities in Afghanistan increasingly handled by HN forces. Continuous American combat operations and homeland defense investments since 2001 have "contributed to resentment abroad and both political controversy and massive fiscal deficit at home."[43] Our elected leaders and other national security professionals wrestle with incessant challenges in their quest for global security, furtherance of democratic values, and our other national security interests. Among present flashpoints, leaders are watching the ongoing adjustments associated with the "Arab Spring"; unfinished revolutions that have increased volatility and uncertainty across both North Africa and the Middle East: some of the most populous and resource rich regions.[44] China's soaring economic and military power, and the belligerent sword-rattling of two third-rate, possibly nuclear powers, North Korea and Iran, is also particularly unsettling for the U.S., western states, and regional neighbors.[45]

One constant of devastating natural disasters, famine, drought, and various refugee crises will continue to demand global responses and, in many cases, U.S. involvement; although frequently challenging and resource intensive, these situations proffer opportunities to bolster our long-term national influence.

The most significant current concern for the U.S. and many other countries, particularly those of the European Union, centers on economics—economies in much of the world are in peril.[46] Private citizens, corporate, and government mismanagement, an imbalance in government revenue versus spending, lackluster growth, and heightened unemployment, have contributed towards a loss in public confidence with both domestic and national foreign policy agendas.[47] Our national economic health has elevated in prominence to the forefront of our national security interests. The global debt crisis increasingly challenges governments' actions and the measures they will undertake to guarantee resolutions within their national interest. A combination of National war-weariness and an era of fiscal austerity will inform U.S. strategic decisions and approaches to both challenges and opportunities.[48] As the 2011 Army Posture Statement indicates, "readiness at best value"[49] will undoubtedly be the new norm as our civilian and military leadership chart our course for National Security Strategy and reshape military capabilities.

Against this backdrop, existing and potential adversaries have closely watched for lessons where countries dared to challenge the U.S. in force-on-force military confrontation. Ghosts from opposing past armies, the Axis Powers during World War II, and the more recent slaughter of Saddam Hussein's forces in both 1991 and 2003 have soberly moderated the zeal others might have to tackle the U.S. in such a direct, conventional fashion.[50] Today the U.S. military remains pre-eminent and should maintain this status for the extended future.[51] The scale, depth, and protracted duration of the increasingly networked form of warfare we have been practicing have also transformed our U.S. joint forces to "finally become truly interdependent."[52] Our joint forces have become increasingly rare; other nations cede that the U.S. is presently the only nation that can operate globally and independently if necessary.[53]

The recent examples of Georgia and Libya suggest that only the U.S. can currently project power in all dimensions.[54] Our closest traditional European allies have already downsized their militaries to the point that they now only exercise and project companies and battalions of mounted maneuver forces rather than brigades and divisions. With continuation along its trajectory of shrinking defense budgets and minimal relevant capabilities, Europe as an entity risks becoming increasingly irrelevant as an actor on the global security stage.[55]

Instead, our adversaries have watched and learned from others that employed alternate, irregular warfare strategies and succeeded in their confrontations with major conventional powers. The Vietnamese bested the French and Americans, the Algerians won against the French, the Afghans wore down the U.S.S.R., Hezbollah bloodied the Israelis in 2006, and the collective insurgencies in Iraq and Afghanistan have at minimum increased the cost the U.S. and its partners paid for negligible results. In each of these cases, the weaker opposition employed strategies and tactics that effectively countered conventional military prowess.[56] Present and future adversaries should be expected to seek to offset our strengths and attack our perceived weaknesses by adapting along these same lines and incorporating increasingly affordable technological solutions, otherwise known as practicing "Asymmetric Warfare."[57]

Enemies that do, or would, employ Asymmetric Warfare against a formidable conventional power would not necessarily fight the same way against a peer or lesser power.[58] To maximize their impact upon their adversary, Army Field Manual 7-0 indicates that practitioners of Asymmetric Warfare will seek to create a "Hybrid Threat" that incorporates a "diverse and dynamic combination of regular forces, irregular forces, criminal elements, or a combination of these forces and elements all unified to achieve mutually benefitting effects."[59] Recent combat experience clearly indicates that well-led and highly trained conventional forces can be decisively defeated in engagements where the enemy employs a broad range of weapon capabilities, ranging from advanced military technology to the application of simple technology used unconventionally. For extended campaigns, hybrid enemies are most successful when they creatively mix and transition between tactics and weapons.[60] In future scenarios where adversaries elect to fight the U.S., we should expect their strategies will include a combination of principles that seek to: control access to the region, change the nature of the conflict, employ operational shielding, control the tempo, neutralize technological overmatch, cause politically unacceptable casualties, and allow no sanctuary.[61]

Our current and prospective opponents include rogue states and a variety of non-state actors—insurgents, guerillas, criminal organizations (including drug cartels), religious extremists, and political groups.[62] In many scenarios, we can expect them to join in "alliances of convenience" to achieve short-term objectives of common interest. Inherently, some groups will have many of these hybrid qualities already within their organization even without collaboration. Furthermore, these syndicates have increasingly networked and created cellular organizational structures to minimize the effectiveness of our targeting.[63]

Hezbollah, during their 2006 war with Israel, and the 2008 terrorist attacks in Mumbai, India, provide salient examples of the terror and wide-ranging effects a relatively small, well-organized, and capable networked group can foment when operating hidden among the population.[64] When they can obtain these assets, hybrid threat adversaries will seek to include modern communications, extended range rockets, unmanned aerial vehicles (UAVs), advanced armor-penetrating weaponry, and anti-access/area-denial (A2/AD) capabilities. Weapons of mass destruction (WMD) are an ultimate goal; most future enemies will seek to obtain them by any means possible, including self-development and production. If obtained, WMD will be used for deterrence, coercion, and strikes at targets locally or in the U.S. and/or allied homelands.[65]

Since our opponents are expected to employ Asymmetric Warfare, the exact nature of our future conflicts resists precise categorization; these conflicts' hallmark will include the opposition's attempt to routinely combine various types of warfare and transition between tactics that historically have been characterized as distinctly different kinds of operations.[66] An appropriate example is Hezbollah's form of hybrid operations during its 2006 war with Israel. Hezbollah had achieved the combined status of simultaneously being a state-sponsored terrorist group, a political movement, a humanitarian relief organization, and a conventional military force. Based on what Israel was confronted with (conventional maneuver, irregular tactics, information warfare, terrorist acts and criminal disorder), and Israel's necessity to continuously react and transition between multiple forms of combat, the U.S. must redouble its efforts to be prepared to rapidly and effectively tackle both high- and low-intensity threats.[67]

In addition to the violence, destruction, and intimidation expected on any battlefield, hybrid threat opponents will also wage Information Operations Campaigns (including deception and propaganda) using all manner of mediums to undercut political and public support for the conflict within the U.S. and internationally. Their themes and messages will seek to portray their version of the "truth and legitimacy" to local, American, and other foreign audiences.[68] In contrast to the U.S. preference for quick, decisive campaigns, future conflicts are much more likely to become protracted affairs, much more akin to "marathons" than our desired "sprints".[69] These enemies will "seek victory through non-defeat and 'disappear' into the local population."[70] Historically, nations sought war outcomes that eliminated the opposition's ability and willingness to continue fighting. In the future, outcomes will increasingly be measured by the residual effects on the populations.[71]

In February 2011, then-Secretary of Defense Robert Gates reminded us that, despite our military prowess, our track record indicates that we should remain cautious of placing much certainty as to the exact location, specific scope, and duration of our next military engagements:

> When it comes to predicting the nature and location of our next military engagements, since Vietnam, our track record has been perfect. We have never once gotten it right, from the Mayaguez to Grenada, Panama, Somalia, the Balkans, Haiti, Kuwait, Iraq, and more—we had no idea a year before any of these missions that we would be so engaged.[72]

Soon after this speech, our military was also committed in Libya. A brief scan of these previous and ongoing operations is significant to inform our preparation for future commitments. U.S. forces will continue to be committed in areas where vital national interests appear to be at risk. Our leaders will also continue to use the U.S. military in situations to meet treaty obligations as well as both formal and informal alliance commitments.[73] Furthermore, we should expect that U.S. forces will be employed in circumstances that are only negligibly or perhaps ambiguously within the Nation's interest.[74]

These previous examples, our past occasional decisions to intervene on the basis of values, such as the right–to-protect (R2P), and opponents' preference to engage us asymmetrically, suggest two key planning considerations: the general battlefield operating environment and the expectation that we will be called to execute the full range of military operations. Combining global trends and enemy initiative, our future operating environment will most commonly be in urban, frequently densely populated, and other complex terrain that offset our U.S. force advantages, as Former Secretary Gates put it, those advantages that give us the "ability to shoot, move and communicate with speed and precision."[75] Nathan Freier from the Center for Strategic and International Studies (CSIS) indicates we should expect both short and long-term operations that span the spectrum of conflict: quick raids and strikes; securing WMD, vital resources, infrastructure, terrain, or freedom of access; regime change; more messy stability operations and counterinsurgency campaigns; building partner capacity; and humanitarian assistance and disaster relief.[76]

In January 2012, President Obama and senior defense officials laid out the framework that will be used to inform our upcoming strategy, capabilities-mix, and the associated force structure. Few, if any, are surprised that the new construct outlining our global presence will increasingly emphasize the Asia-Pacific while sustaining a close watch on the Middle East and the capabilities for military engagement there, when and if required. The new framework does direct a substantial change, directly impacting the Army and the Marine Corps, in that "U.S. forces will no longer be sized to conduct large-scale, prolonged Stability Operations." In other areas of the world, particularly outside of Asia-Pacific and Middle East, we will seek to primarily sustain our influence through a whole-of-government approach that aims to maintain our defense commitments, strengthen alliances and partnerships, builds partner capacity, and increases regional security.

In what is stated as the "blueprint for the Joint Force of 2020, the President emphasized the importance of deepening partnerships with our like-minded friends. Working with the other elements of our national power, DOD will play key major roles in military-to-military (or wider with other security forces) relationships. Through specific engagements, episodic exercises, and programs the U.S. can bolster regional security, American influence, partner capacity, our interoperability, and increase the number of friends that serve as "security exporters" rather than "security consumers."[77] In line with this announcement, in a December 2011 *Armed Forces Journal* article, Robert Killebrew indicated that "expeditionary warfare" by U.S. troops engaging in combat as should remain an option, but the least preferred course of action. Instead, the U.S. should work with, train, and otherwise resource friends to do the heavy-lifting in their establishing control over ungoverned territories and their own defense. For the U.S., such a strategy is "cost-effective defense." Our warriors must embrace military assistance, but also be prepared to deploy on short-notice and fight to win on arrival.[78]

In this increasingly complex and dangerous security environment, the Army's Capstone Concept (TRADOC Pamphlet 525-3-0) indicates that our joint forces will confront adversaries that employ hybrid threats while inter-dispersed amongst complicated indigenous populations with different cultures, political, religious norms and motivations; the "fog and friction of war persists."[79] Both state and non-state adversaries are more likely to have and use capabilities to challenge us, within the combat theater and outside of it, in multiple domains (land, sea, air, space, and cyber).[80] Domestic and international legitimacy for military action, in most instances, especially when involvement is likely to include extended periods of U.S. "boots-on-the-ground," we will actively seek to act within a coalition of like-minded partners. Our success, particularly in all types of Irregular Warfare and Stability Operations, will depend on having leaders at all levels work effectively with and through an increasingly broad array of "agencies and organizations—government, intergovernmental, nongovernmental, and commercial—and usually within a multinational military framework."[81]

The Future Strategic Security Environment's Meaning for U.S. Landpower

In view of the ongoing evolution of the strategic security environment, what ground force capabilities are most relevant for the future? Although our national leadership intends to place the greater strategic focus on the Asia-Pacific, this, in

20

actuality, does not decrease the importance of U.S. "Landpower" (the Army, Marine Corps and special operations forces)[82]—with the Army as the cornerstone of these ground forces. On February 24, 2012 at the Association of the U.S. Army's (AUSA) Winter Symposium, the Chief of Staff of the Army, General Raymond Odierno indicated that "AirSea" is a contingency operation and "certainly not a new DOD strategy." An expeditionary Army remains crucial to the priority missions, deterring and defeating aggression.[83]

The other domains of U.S. military power will not be able to secure the nation's objectives alone. Among others, a 2009 RAND study led by David Johnson indicates that hybrid opponents demand "a joint, combined-arms approach that enables integrated fire and maneuver, particularly in complex terrain and in military operations among the people."[84] Even if ground forces are not used as our primary military instruments in the Asia-Pacific region, ground forces will play a crucial role in deterring conflict elsewhere and keeping those crises that erupt manageable. A robust ground force capability, with the BCT as the basic element of our combined arms and maneuver formations, will remain in constant demand for at least the next ten years. Nathan Freier's 2011 study indicates that any strategy that ignores the continued, if not heightened, relevancy of ground forces that can be rapidly committed and dominate the operational environment is bankrupt; such strategies will soon be found to have posed unacceptable constraints on policymakers' ability to shape and deliver favorable foreign policy outcomes.[85]

Despite the fact that our leadership will seek to avoid, whenever possible, involving U.S. troops in protracted stability and irregular warfare conflicts, as is frequently said, "the enemy always gets a vote." The realities of our manpower-intensive era of persistent irregular conflict cannot be wished away; for these reasons and more, our ground forces' unique contributions will remain central to any viable U.S. defense strategy or policy options.[86] David Johnson's RAND study indicates that among the warfighting domains, ground forces face the greatest challenges in preparing for their employment in multiple forms of warfare.[87] Andrew Krepinevich from the Center for Strategic and Budgetary Assessments (CSBS) adds that besides the broad array of likely missions and associated tasks that ground forces will be called on to perform, landpower success is much more centric versus the other Services' weighted reliance on systems and materiel.[88] Colonel Gian Gentile, Director of the Military History Program at West Point, believes the future demands a careful, more sophisticated adaptation of U.S. military ground capabilities to cover the messier forms of warfare that we have been decisively engaged with over the last decade as well as the traditional MCO-type scenarios.[89] We must expect that we will be faced with circumstances that demand ground forces that are capable of contested forcible entry deployment into austere theaters and joint capability to sustain operations within non-linear battle space. Our forces should expect to confront multiple adversaries, normally hidden within the population, in countries with little or no state control.[90]

Krepinevich indicates that Stability Operations in places like Nigeria and Pakistan have the potential to be as difficult as or even worse than what we have experienced in Iraq and Afghanistan.[91] In the wake of the Arab Spring revolutions, an alternate, but very plausible scenario finds U.S. forces in Egypt. The U.S. would almost certainly commit ground forces if the larger international community was denied passage through the

Suez Canal. And, although the U.S. will need to sustain the capabilities and depth for Stability Operations and to build-up like-minded friends through Security Force Assistance, Freier's analysis points that "traditional warfighting" competence and the capabilities that heavy formations provide will be both increasingly unique globally and essential for a wide range of contingencies.[92] Armored maneuver forces (e.g., armored and armor-protected infantry and tanks) will remain more important than many envision.[93] Although armored maneuver forces are unlikely to be frequently employed in the massed armies type of scenarios for which they were originally designed, our recent combat experience has proven that the firepower and protection inherent with these maneuver units is also crucial for ground force success in the majority of the operations will face.[94]

Even if as John Nagl of the Center for a New American Security (CNAS) suggests that the Army can expect to be "called upon to more frequently counter insurgencies, intervene in civil strife and humanitarian crisis, rebuild nations, and wage unconventional types of warfare than it is to fight mirror-image armed forces,"[95] there are several very dangerous scenarios that demand high-intensity, MCO capabilities. Gentile indicates that North Korean and Iranian contingencies both provide possibilities where we must be prepared for contested force projection and fight at all levels of the conflict spectrum.[96] For those that believe that the world has progressed beyond fast-moving conventional armies facing-off, recall the 2008 situation where Georgian infantry was under intense fire from advancing Russian armor formations.[97]

A final, yet equally poignant reason to maintain heavy capabilities goes back to the central tenet of Asymmetric Warfare; Krepinevich warns that if we yield our dominant position, our adversaries will fill this gap by fielding conventional forces that can further threaten our interests.[98] This Russian-Georgian War was also the first known where at least one of the warring parties (Russia in this case) allegedly made coordinated attacks on its adversary in the cyber domain at the same time it engaged in the land, air, sea, and space domains. The alleged Russian cyber attacks targeted "54 web sites in Georgia related to communications, finance, and the government ...So as tanks and troops were crossing the border and bombers were flying sorties, Georgian citizens could not access web sites for information or instructions."[99] As such the Russian-Georgian War is an example of our traditional conventional war that added the asymmetric "cyber" twist.

As our leadership ponders what balance and mix are truly required within the joint force, history offers lessons. Considering all capabilities the other U.S. Services contribute, only forward deployed ground forces signal our ultimate commitment, reassuring allies and partners while at the same time serving as warning to our collective enemies; as Freier indicates within *U.S. Ground Force Capabilities through 2020*, "the resolve and willingness to put American men and women shoulder to shoulder with the populations of foreign partners in harm's way."[100] Our decision makers should also study the dangerous lesson Israel learned in 2006 which showed that strategic failure can be the price if an army focuses too narrowly on preparing forces exclusively for counterinsurgency and constabulary–type missions. Over a nearly thirty year period, Israel primarily focused on low-intensity counterinsurgency; even with ample combat experience, they were unprepared for the hybrid warfare Hezbollah elected to fight.[101] Of course, our own experiences in Iraq and Afghanistan indicate the opposite also yields untenable consequences.

To hedge against the reality that we will not be able to accurately predict the exact time, place, or nature of our future military interventions, our total force must be well-led, appropriately trained, flexible and adaptive in nature, postured for rapid deployment, and ready for all manner of contingencies. Despite the upcoming force and resource reductions, Colonel Scott Efflandt argued in a 2010 *Military Review* article that our future recalibrated Army must be built on the premise of cohesive units—units that are well prepared for high and low-intensity operations and capable of simultaneously shifting their approach as the situation alters.[102] Building tactical formations that are ready for such challenges requires that units develop skills, experience, and teamwork; if this is done in combat instead of during training, the price can be extremely high in terms of lives and lost opportunities.

The U.S. ground forces' situation today in terms of our readiness to face potential new challenges bears many similarities to what the Israeli Defense Forces (IDF) faced in 2006. The IDF was very proficient and experienced with COIN when their Hezbollah opponent, employing hybrid tactics, handed them a very messy and embarrassing surprise. What the IDF faced in Lebanon reinforces the fact that extensive combat experience in one form of warfare does not translate to a force's universal effectiveness.[103] Their 2006 experience also reminds us that high-intensity combat "is not so much about scale (i.e., battalion or brigade force-on-force engagements) as about the qualitative challenges a hybrid threat can pose."[104] The IDF did recover from this setback through their subsequent refocus towards restoring high-intensity, combined-arms capabilities; this blending of combined-arms capabilities with their Irregular Warfare expertise produced very satisfactory and much improved performance against their hybrid opponents in Gaza during 2008.[105] The IDF's success in re-tooling their units is good news for the U.S. With the American exit from Iraq and expected continued troop reductions in Afghanistan, the U.S. is rapidly approaching a point where most of our BCTs can allocate the time and energy required to prepare for FSO; this game plan will work for us too.

<u>The Army's Current Vector as Part of Joint Force 2020</u>

The Army is adjusting its doctrine, organization, and the way it intends to prepare for its expected future responsibilities, including the new normal of dealing with hybrid threats. The primary challenge is, that the future recalibrated Army must be, as the January 2012 U.S. Defense Strategy indicates, "agile, flexible, and ready for the full range of contingencies"[106] even as we undergo significant force and resource reductions. Senior military leaders and the defense academic community have been evaluating the ends, ways, means, and risks associated with developing the correct type of Army for years.

Our doctrine and warfighting construct is now catching up to modern realities; this current doctrine is centered on our force preparing for and executing FSO (i.e. simultaneous offensive, defensive, and stability or support operations).[107] Leading this Army doctrinal rewrite, Lieutenant General William Caldwell noted that our "future is not one of major battles and engagements fought by armies on battlefields devoid of population; instead, the course of conflict will be decided by forces operating among the people of the world."[108]

Unlike preceding constructs, this version places equal emphasis on having units prepare for each type of operation and recognizes that they are rarely separate events.[109] In many circumstances, MCO or IW (offensive or defensive) will be occurring in close proximity to limited Stability Operations. Soldiers from the same units will be applying lethal and non-lethal combat power while executing aspects of all FSO competencies, sometimes transitioning between them several times in a single day.[110] This doctrine will place a premium on having leaders, Soldiers, and units that are comfortable with making decisions in situations with ill-defined problems; demonstrating a high degree of "operational adaptability".[111]

After evaluating the options of what force construct would be employed to execute this doctrine, the Army's leadership recognized that neither America's elected leaders nor the taxpayers would presently bankroll large ground forces that are tailored for specific forms of warfare. The resulting decision is that the Army will concentrate on fielding more flexible units—a "full-spectrum force."[112] For the Army units that comprise the BCT, as well as other Army and JIIM partners that operate within a BCT's battle space, the challenges associated with preparation for FSO in the 21st century are daunting.

In summary, the present and forecasted strategic environment of Joint Force 2020 is increasingly interconnected, and one of emerging state and non-state actors that will vie for power, influence, and privileges on a regional and even global basis. In many cases, these actors' objectives will run cross-purposes with U.S. interests. The strategic environment is increasingly hostile to U.S. involvement in many forms. The U.S. military forces remain preeminent, but national economic debt and the resulting reduction in defense–related expenditures and national war weariness are some of the challenges that confront face the Joint Force.

Informed by over seventy years of historical lessons, actual and prospective adversaries have determined that when physically challenging the U.S. military, the odds favor those who employ asymmetric methods. As such, most adversaries will incorporate a combination of methods and tactics, also referred to as the "hybrid threat" throughout campaigns against the U.S. Hybrid enemies will execute a kaleidoscope of traditional approaches incorporating conventional, irregular, and clandestine actions as well as influencing operations designed to counter actual or perceived U.S. advantages and the U.S. and global public opinion. Where possible, adversaries will attack the U.S., allies, and friends, employing all domains and making every effort to take the fight to our homelands. The broad span of possible global U.S. force commitments, coupled with resource limitations, preclude extensive niche capability specialization, thus requiring the Army to field a "full-spectrum force."

During the AUSA's February 2012 Winter Symposium, Major General Frederick Hodges, the Army's Chief of Legislative Liaison, aptly captured landpower's enduring relevance when he indicated "there is a lot of blue in the Pacific theater, but they do not live in the blue…they live in the greens and the browns."[113] General Dempsey indicates that the force's success in the future requires that our formations are "proficient in more than combat, and must remain versatile to conduct security, engagement, relief and reconstruction."[114] He also emphasizes that ground forces proficiency within MCO (as well as in the tasks, skills, more closely associated with other forms of operations) atrophies without routine practice.[115] Without doubt, the present force possesses extensive combat experience and demonstrated abilities at adapting under a diverse array of complex and stress-packed situations; however, to avoid repetition of the unwelcome reality check that the Israeli's experienced in 2006, our leaders, Soldiers, and units must also be able to blend MCO competencies within their portfolio of Irregular Warfare and Stability Operations prowess.

The Army's future deployed missions will be predominantly conducted in a JIIM operating environment—in densely populated urbanized and other complex terrain. In these locations, and others that have yet to require large U.S. commitments to ground combat, our nation will place increasing weight towards working "by, with, and through" partners in order to shape the international environment designed to achieve the desired strategic outcomes. The Army's institutional training base, represented in part by the NTC, faces a major challenge in order to provide BCTs, and other units that benefit from NTC rotations, the optimal pre-deployment training and readiness validation prior to engaging in actual FSO.

Optimizing NTC for Army 2020

Over recent years, the NTC has achieved an as yet unprecedented level of fidelity in the specifically tailored operational environments it has generated in training units for their Afghanistan and Iraq commitments. NTC rotations have traditionally played major roles in providing our RTUs the unique experiences judged essential prior to their foreign commitments to "assist friends, reassure and protect populations, and identify, isolate, and defeat enemies."[116] In preparation for the Army's future global challenges and to "restore the balance" in force readiness for full-spectrum operations, what NTC adaptations might be necessary in order that our units can "train as they are expected to fight?" Capstone CTC training must incorporate additional hurdles that lead units to exercise different muscle groups. Without modification, the existing NTC COE portrayal lacks sufficient infrastructure, texture, atmospherics, and signatures to serve as an adequate canvas for exercising the breadth and depth of updated full-spectrum doctrine. Before implementing another series of partially synchronized adjustments at the NTC, I suggest that the Army leadership should undertake an unconstrained look at the past rotations can contribute to high-payoff and high-end collective proficiency. The future NTC COE constructs should continue to do so through relevant design that is packed with challenges for the troops.

To better represent many potential operations, the training battle space should represent portions of at least two countries; one of them being a hostile state that has already, or nearly, commenced combat with a struggling U.S. ally. Within an array of opponents employing hybrid tactics, a portion of the enemy force should possess advanced conventional capabilities. Training scenarios should lead to requirements for the RTUs to execute forced or contested entry operations and subsequently expand the lodgments. At the beginning of the rotation, U.S. units should not simply occupy pre-prepared Forward Operating Bases (FOBs) that are just waiting for units to arrive and assume operations; instead, these units will require a more "expeditionary" mindset versus the "rotational" one where U.S. units essentially execute a relief-in-place or transition-of-authority with their U.S. predecessors. Future rotations should incorporate threats, such as the possibility of air and missile attack, that U.S. ground forces have not been seriously challenged with for years. Also added to the opposition's order-of-battle are offensive cyber capabilities and efforts that seek to degrade our space-based technological advantages. Far from returning to the largely austere and sterile maneuver training areas used to prepare earlier generations, the FSO training environment must continue to build upon the measures the NTC employed to train units for Afghanistan and Iraq.[117]

The basic components that will enable the diverse range of required training experiences rely on having an authentic physical environment and heavy emphasis on the human interaction. The NTC COE must showcase an entangled mix of friendly, neutral, and opposition (conventional and irregular) elements inhabiting urban and other complex terrain.[118] As depicted, the interwoven societal dynamics should include: foreign language, culture, religion, and sectarian or tribal issues; a government apparatus that is locked in a struggle for legitimacy; other political undercurrents; security forces; visible economics and commerce that includes small businesses and industry, services, transportation, and agriculture; modern information technology and the media; offensive cyber capabilities; and both criminal and insurgent activity. Besides convincingly portraying the indigenous population and any coalition allies, the NTC COE must challenge our BCTs to deal with all manner of other civilian third-party actors found on 21st century battlefields including, among others, humanitarian relief agencies, other international governmental organizations, the news media, and refugees.[119]

Collective enhancements to the present NTC COE portrayal of the physical and human terrain will provide the necessary backdrop for leaders and Soldiers in honing their collective abilities to anticipate change, identify opportunities, and take prudent risk. Adhering to the Army's updated doctrinal principles, this interactive and controlled training environment should be inundated with a mixture of ill-defined and ambiguous conditions that will provide units the experience and confidence needed to seize, retain, and exploit the initiative and master transitions between operational themes.[120]

Aligned within new doctrine, NTC's COE exercise design must provide units with ample opportunities to demonstrate basic small-to-large combined arms operations, to include the integration of both organic and joint fires and enablers. The rotations must also sustain emphasis on fundamental lessons from our Afghanistan and Iraq experience, as well as observations from both Lebanon and Georgia, which are likely to be equally important across the range of future U.S. landpower commitments. Although the military should concentrate on its enemy in all forms of warfare, many past, ongoing, and future operations suggest that more of the Army's, and wider JIIM, efforts should be "population centric," by doing so, we are both more likely to deny opponents their objectives and more rapidly attain favorable outcomes.

Accordingly, the rotational scenarios should inject situations that, as the *Army Operating Concept* prescribes, drive leaders and Soldiers to demonstrate their ability to "develop an understanding of the situation through action in close contact with the enemy and the civil population"[121] and then, accordingly, continually adjust operations. By employing well-crafted scenarios, NTC should generate requirements at multiple echelons that thoroughly test the RTU's abilities to appreciate local cultural norms and interact in a non-English speaking environment, maintain fire power restraint, undertake civic action programs in collaboration with other parties, operate (and perhaps integrate) with local security forces, serve as advisors, and provide security and other forms of support to reconstruction efforts.[122]

Providing a NTC experience is dependent on exercise design and a variety of resources (manning, equipping, training areas, support, simulation and the associated funding). The NTC's leadership molds all elements to generate realistic manifestations of the COE in order to produce certain training outcomes.[123] With any operational environment, the COE is the composite of "operational variables" (Political, Military, Economic, Social, Information, Infrastructure, Physical Environment, and Time [PMESII-PT]).[124] After evaluating a variety of possibilities, I suggest that NTC should target most emphasis towards select "operational variables" in order to generate the training conditions most appropriate for training the Army of 2020. Additional adjustments to what the present "box" portrays in terms of the Infrastructure, Social, and Economic variables can collectively make a major advance towards transforming the battlefield to one that optimally portrays unified land operations within a RTU's battle space. In doing so, the COE's complexity and human interaction can portray a level of fidelity that, as General Martin Dempsey suggests, thoroughly challenges Soldiers' "interaction with the terrain, the population, and the enemy."[125]

Recognizing the fiscal austerity that is expected to continue, I also present ideas on how NTC can approach exercise design changes "smarter." By incorporating various assets and financial resources to incrementally adjust the COE, the Army and taxpayers can reduce the overall cost these changes would require if contracted through the private sector. Although NTC COE adjustment to better replicate the emerging threats in the space and cyber space domains are also necessary, I lack the expertise to make recommendations that adequately tackle these highly technical challenges.

The NTC's COE Infrastructure Variable

In order to transform the box to reflect the type of urban and complex terrain appropriate for the Army's 2020 COE, NTC should reevaluate its box "Master Plan" and assign a qualified team that have long-term longevity to serve synchronize and integrate adjustments for the future. To be successful in this endeavor, NTC needs reexamine the box without the "range-control" sort of management lens. The box planning team should include licensed engineers, architects, city or county planners, and others skilled in manipulating the Army's bureaucratic processes to collectively integrate possible options with changing windows of available resources (units to provide specialized and non-specialized labor, materials, etc.).

The first major project to transform the box should be the construction of at least one international border. As part of this effort, a variety of adjustments are required, to include: permanent or semi-permanent border crossing points with infrastructure on both sides of the border; associated customs, immigration, and border controls; and permanent border defenses or barriers on both sides (examples: tank ditches, mine fields, berms, vehicle fighting positions, dragon's teeth, and guard towers). Adding the international border will generate a variety of second and third-order effects that challenge the coalition with dealing with international incidents and cross-border issues (air and ground), to include appropriately dealing with acts-of-war. By limiting the amount of the box that is used to depict our allied state, NTC can mitigate other challenges in terms of resources. As such, most of the time, the majority of role players can be concentrated in a smaller portion of the box, better amplifying the population density expected with urban operations. Additionally, with a reduced area of the box, the available capital resources can be concentrated over the reduced footprint.

The second major addition appropriate to Army 2020 is establishing at least one airfield that is C-130 capable, with civilian airport infrastructure. An airfield is important for exercising expected challenges associated with a variety of missions to include forced-entry operations and sustaining the force.

Most future operations will likely include situations where there will be refugee requirements for their respective national governments. Coalition forces will likely have a role in providing some sort of assistance or stabilizing presence, as will International Organizations (IOs) and other Non-governmental Organizations (NGOs). Incorporating refugee camps on both sides of the border will further enhance expected real-world conditions.

A majority of the urban construction has relied on MILVAN container-based buildings that have had windows and doors added and stucco-type exterior finish added. These container buildings are reminiscent of two-dimensional movie sets that are convincing from the frontal view only. Most are neither big enough in the height or depth to provide appropriate replication of the functions the structures are intended to represent. This type of construction, stucco and wire mesh used on building exteriors and less resilient town walls, does not stand up to the harsh environmental conditions of the Mojave Desert or the wear-and-tear of simulated combat operations. There are far too few walled compounds that are prevalent in the COE and remain appropriate to training our forces on targeting and raids. When considering future urban construction, master planners should emphasize solid better-built structures over reliance on MILVAN container buildings. Cinder block or wooden structures can be constructed by skilled and non-skilled role player labor during actual rotations. Adopting this approach reduces overall cost for additional structures, produces more appropriate facilities that will better withstand the environment and heavy wear-and-tear, and deepens the COE's economic and social signatures. In addition to multi-story buildings most towns and rural areas should have a greatly increased number of concrete or rock masonry walls.

The main roads in the training area need to be paved; doing so is not out-of-character with most of the world and doing so provides numerous benefits to enhance authenticity and off-sets costs associated with vehicle wear-and-tear. This adjustment would greatly improve traffic circulation and assist with vehicle issues as well as safety. Much of the labor for this project could be executed by military units for the cost of their TDY and materials. While the paving project was ongoing, it would also increase the number of role players and add appropriate economic signatures.

Fort Irwin is presently building a solar array that will be used to power the installation and sell excess power to the surrounding area. The box should benefit from the installation's increased electrical capacity and power lines run to all the towns. Local electrical sub-stations (actual or replicas) should also be added to increase replication of key-infrastructure.

Another area of key infrastructure that can be incorporated to promote a variety of security actions is building a simulated pipe-line across a portion of the box. Similar to road work by military engineers, this mock-pipeline could be built by Army fuel specialists for the price of the materials. Since the pipeline would not need to actually function, it could be constructed with mainly reclaimed piping and materials. Viable additions to the pipeline could include adding non-functioning oil-field structures such as oil-wells that should be able to be obtained at the cost of transportation.

Although it is situated in a desert, the box has a distinct absence of vegetation and agriculture that would accompany at least portions of actually populated regions; both are representative of local economies and commerce and also drive units to undertake expanded missions and tasks not yet adequately trained. NTC can make great improvements in these areas, increase the variety on forms of training tasks and challenges for the RTU, and if carefully planned, do so in a manner that should be affordable. Additional vegetation will assist with mitigating sand and wind issues that plague town appearance, maintenance, and quality of life for role player residents. Further, increased vegetation and agriculture along roads and main supply routes is authentic in most regions. It adds opportunities for the OPFOR and increases the challenge for the RTU and HN security forces. To optimize the likelihood that vegetation not only survives but also prospers in the box, most items selected for planting should be those that grow naturally in this environment or similar ones that need minimal care and maintenance after planting.[126] For watering, obtain water from the existing non-potable wells vicinity of Madina Jabal and distribute using current water tankers.

Actual agriculture should also be incorporated at several locations within the box. NTC could employ the same sort of contracting techniques used on other installations that permit farmers and ranchers to use training areas. As part of the agreement, NTC could agree provide the necessary water and electrical power for the farming and daily transportation for workers between the box and main post. At least some of the fields should be irrigated and there could be one or more canal network incorporated. Possible orchards that should be considered for this addition include cultivation with olive, citrus, and pear trees, eucalyptus and fruit trees (including the Date Palm). Other

37

crops considered should include barley, wheat, corn, sunflowers, and rice. Successfully incorporating additional vegetation and agriculture to the COE would be a major improvement to the depth and complexity of the social and economic dynamics which units normally face when deployed. It would also add additional working population to bolster the number of civilians in the box.

The NTC's COE Social Variable

This paper differentiates the "Social Variable" between two different components, those that are part of the wider RTU and those that represent the rest of the population to include HN security forces and the opposition. The present COE lacks is sufficient depth in the non-RTU population. With about 2,200[127] people in non-RTU roles compared an average of 6,228[128] RTU participants, the population is spread too thin to regularly generate the volume of interaction and the societal dynamics of a COE province.

NTC should build upon the level of JIIM participation that is normal in current MREs. As often as possible, the JIIM interaction should be performed by rotational participants from the other services, interagency, and foreign partners. When this is not possible, NTC needs to contract for professional role players who have the background and experience for authentic free-play interaction with the RTU and other scenario stakeholders. Former international military officers, State Department and U.S. AID officials, including retirees, are good candidates to provide the required level of fidelity to these key roles.

As an addition to current practices, the rotational "troop list" should also incorporate a light-heavy mix into each rotation so that all parties must work through the special challenges inherent with employing and sustaining these different capabilities.

For a Heavy or Stryker BCT, at least a light company-sized force should be attached; vice versa for an Infantry BCT. In addition to the role players that portray HN security forces and some coalition presence, future rotations should also include greater "live" partner participation. Future troop lists should include company or battalion-sized allied units and sufficient liaison officers to assist integrate them into combined operations. If partner nations cannot outright fund their own transportation and participation, the Army should examine a combination of exercise and Acquisition Cross-Servicing Agreement (ACSA) funding streams.

With my discussion about instituting international borders, this paper already covered the advantages that decreasing the amount of the box that NTC routinely attempts to populate and generate traffic and other commerce between towns and villages. Bringing military engineering units to NTC for select projects and having them work in civilian clothes is another way to add to the civilian population. The example I used detailing adding agriculture to the box demonstrates another mechanism to employ on obtaining non-military and non-government funded contractors to add to the box's resident population. To add additional depth to the intense societal dynamics and saturate the box with an appropriate number of people, the Army needs to re-implement its pre-2003 practice that tasked additional units to participate in each NTC rotation. These units could be easily incorporated into providing portions of the HN security forces and conventional OPFOR. Employing additional units in this manner would provide them with outstanding core training and allow NTC to more accurately depict the depth and breadth of the COE.

The NTC's COE Economic Variable

Training and Doctrine Command Circular (TC) 7-101, *Exercise Design*, indicates the economic variable "encompasses individual and group behaviors related to producing, distributing, and consuming resources."[129] The NTC's present COE economic depiction lacks sufficient complex challenges that the RTU should encounter in order to dissect the layers of problems and opportunities associated with societal dynamics.[130] Better integration of the four economic sub-variables (economic diversity, employment status, illegal economic activity, and banking and finance)[131] with the other PMESII-PT operational variables will better demonstrate the reason the population exist within the battle space and appropriately reflect the underpinnings of a functioning society. When considering how to adjust the economic and social variables to more appropriately replicate an indigenous society, NTC should seek adjustments that collectively transform the recent COE from essentially only coming to life when the RTU has elements in town to one that has all manner of activity occurring constantly, everywhere, and that activity is only slightly based on RTU physical presence.

The NTC must broadly examine the reason the COE's population lives in the box and analyze where and how it can produce the signatures and undercurrents associated with legal and illicit economic activity that can include a variety of mechanisms associated with manufacturing, agriculture, mining, trade, distribution, and the service sector.[132] This paper has already introduced recommendations on expanding replication of portions of the economic variable to include HN security forces, civilian airport operations, relief workers, as well as the agricultural, construction, and oil industries. There are numerous additional opportunities to account for normal activity within the box that can be incrementally added or modified to generate enhanced plausible scenario constructs that incorporate the following: local governance, administration, public and social services, in addition to representing commodity transfer across established distribution networks. Comprehensive execution will generate a realistic volume of labor at practiced occupations with the commensurate vehicular and pedestrian traffic as role players move constantly in a purposeful manner throughout the box executing their occupational, family, or nefarious responsibilities as the "bad guys."

Some additional recommended areas for NTC to examine in order to better represent the economic variable include role player operated businesses and establishments that actually perform a variety of functions. From the governmental sector there should be government offices, police stations, prisons, fire departments, hospitals and clinics, a postal system, mosques (and/or churches) and cemeteries, schools, and military installations. NTC should expand its commercial and service sector portrayal to incorporate small manufacturing and industry such as mining and furniture manufacturing, open-air markets to include shoe-shine men and other types of mobile vendors, shops and stores, agricultural supply stores, construction material businesses, painting contractors, gas stations and garages, and auto dealerships. There should also be banks and money lenders, restaurants and cafes, hotels, internet cafes, public utilities and associated infrastructure, as well as newspapers and radio stations. In addition to the portrayal of privately owned vehicles circulating the road networks, the box should also have functioning bus lines, trucking firms, taxis, and a selection of farm machinery transiting between various locations. This diverse range of plausible and busy urban and rural dynamics affords the societal complexity appropriate for masking black market activities for a variety of commodities and other types of crime and insurgent activities that can include smuggling, kidnapping, theft, as well as narcotics and/or explosive device production, stockpiling, and distribution. Such a backdrop will provide the RTU a tremendous challenge at successfully executing its varied responsibilities across the range of operations.

How to Provide Enhanced Realism at Reduced Cost

There are a number of underexplored possibilities and avenues to examine in greater detail in order for NTC to replicate a more accurate depiction of the COE that Army and JIIM forces will operate in up to 2020 and beyond. Earlier, this paper highlighted the importance of incorporating a well-resourced team of master planners to coordinate the continuous improvement of the box; such an entity is essential to working through the many short and long-term options as part of a three to six-year plan that can truly transform the box into a sustained legacy as an unmatched venue for training against the hybrid-threats comprising current and future operations. What more can be done with existing military assets? Instead of continuing to expend large financial outlays by contracting with civilian firms to construct various new physical infrastructure, DOD can employ its own assets to achieve the same effects at a much more affordable cost. Active and reserve component units (Army engineers, Navy Seabees, and Air Force Red Horse units) should be used to build a much greater portion of the future infrastructure. Army petroleum specialists, as stated earlier, and even military and other government civilian communications and network specialists, can be employed to build the infrastructure and connectivity appropriate for the box.

Although the OPFOR (11th ACR) does have one combat engineering company assigned, this unit lacks the necessary specialties and equipment to capitalize on the range of construction capabilities inherent within other engineer unit variants. A heavy engineer company with the expertise for vertical and horizontal construction should be added to the 11th ACR. This unit must also be provided with commercial heavy-equipment better suited for the construction missions called for in the box's COE. 11th ACR Soldiers from non-engineer specialties should be used for the bulk of the manual labor required to construct buildings, walls, and other infrastructure projects throughout the box. This becomes not only affordable, but feasible, if targeted reserve component personnel (electricians, plumbers, and general contractors) with the requisite civilian licensing and credentials are brought onto active duty at NTC to serve as trainers, construction site supervisors, and quality control inspectors.

Another way to increase the Army's, and thus NTC's, organic capability to vastly improve the box's authentic COE portrayal is to increase the non-Military Occupational Specialty (MOS) skills that assigned 11th ACR Soldiers possess. A relatively inexpensive way this can be accomplished is that, in return for a two to one stabilization with the 11th ACR, Soldiers could be given up to six months of permissive TDY to obtain civilian training relevant for role player occupations. Training and certification in areas such as civilian construction, automotive mechanics, specific languages, and some other areas could be funded by each Soldier's G.I. Bill. Individual Soldiers who take advantage of such a program would enhance their post-military employment opportunities with specialized training and extensive practical application of these skills.

As addressed previously, the Army should reinstitute practices that task additional units to participate in each NTC rotation, attached to the 11th ACR, in order to field the appropriate opposing conventional enemy forces, HN security forces, population, and insurgency. Such a construct is a win-win for all parties; it provides the tasked units with invaluable additional training experiences that are presently not achievable at home-stations while also adding to the realism that NTC's exercise design is able to deliver to RTUs. A change in Army policy could require new junior grade Defense Language Institute (DLI) Arabic Course graduates to serve with the 11th ACR for one year before being reassigned to other organizations. This would greatly expand the NTC's ability to provide Soldier role players in language and culturally dependent civilian roles. The Army should also reevaluate the size of the OPFOR (11th ACR) to determine if additional strength increases to this undersized brigade is more cost effective than continuing to augment the number of 11th ACR Soldiers fielded in each rotation with civilian contractors. NTC should also reconsider what other existing activities could be moved from main post into the box in order to generate increased population, more functioning businesses, and increased traffic circulation. These activities could include moving the existing contracted "civilian on the battlefield vehicle" (COBV) motor pool and maintenance facility, the post dental clinic, the dump, and the recycling facility from garrison into the box.

There are additional avenues that NTC should explore in order to get the highest benefits during an era that is expected to pose ever increasing fiscal resource constraints. To pull-in additional non-DOD resources, the NTC planning team needs to consider the core question: which non-DOD entities can possibly benefit from assisting with resourcing NTC's COE in the realms of personnel, subject-matter-expertise, donations of materials, and/or operations and maintenance costs? Group brainstorming sessions backed-up by legal advice can produce a wide array of opportunities for NTC to leverage.

Within the government realm, through the Army, NTC should be able to at least capture small multi-agency (DOS, USAID, CIA, NSA, FBI, and others) financial contributions in return for the benefits these other stakeholders receive from participating in NTC rotations or using the box out-of-cycle. Other portions of the civilian sector, particularly academia and NGOs, can also benefit through partnerships with NTC. Consider NTC's current practice of teaming with universities to find journalism students to serve as members of the media during rotations as a model.[133] The box offers great possibilities as a venue where organizations, universities, and technical training courses can be incorporated to either increase the role player population, with individuals possessing specialized skills, and/or serve as a project laboratory where NTC's COE reaps long-term benefits from their enhancements to the replicated infrastructure and economy.

This paper addressed military-corporate partnerships in the earlier agricultural example as a mechanism that can increase the number of civilian role players into rotations and depict actual societal economics in return for profiting from the box's natural resources. Beyond agriculture, the NTC should seek corporate partnerships that develop and operate small industry with at least cement works, mines, and quarries. In 2008, NTC's commander, then-Brigadier General Dana Pittard, proposed another partnership possibility by enlisting Hollywood studios: in return for their help in building state-of-the-art urban blocks, the studios would have coordinated box access to film.[134]

The final recommendation is likely the easiest for NTC's master planners to implement and provides great pay-back in terms of transforming the NTC COE to reflect more authentic PMESII-PT operational variable signatures. Throughout the US, corporations, businesses, and private citizens possess unneeded or even abandoned vehicles, aircraft, machinery, buildings, and furnishings that would be very suitable to incorporate into the NTC COE. In most, used or reclaimed items work as well if not better than new items to replicate the COE. For tax credits or other mechanisms, NTC could obtain such items, which would otherwise be prohibitively expensive, essentially free.

Conclusion

American units deserve to receive the best training possible before they are committed in harm's way. The hybrid threats Americans should expect to face up to 2020 and beyond will rarely place U.S. and allied land forces on barren and austere battlefields; instead, American Soldiers and their partners will be required to interact with countless stakeholders, normally in densely populated areas and other complex terrain. Training must be informed by the lessons of Afghanistan, Iraq, Lebanon, Georgia, and other past commitments while, concurrently, meshed with the changes expected on future battlefields. These scenarios must generate tests at the edge of RTU capabilities to "prevent" adversaries from escalating conflicts, "shape" the international environment, and, where challenged, "win" decisively and dominantly.[135] The Army should not expect to have rotational exercise design that captures the "mirror-image" of every challenge across the range of operations; however, training should be inclusive enough and close enough to maintain its relevance in generating FSO competencies. The tactical-level prowess, agility, and adaptability such training generates will ensure that strategic decision makers possess the full range of options to safeguard and secure national interests.

Colonel Butch Kievenaar's comments after leading his BCT through a 2008 NTC rotation highlight the enduring value of the CTCs:

> You really can't train yourself. Although we train at home station, we don't have the assets to do the simulations that can be done here, and here I can train the whole brigade at one time, not just elements of it. We really couldn't do this without the CTCs.[136]

Other major armies envy the U.S. maneuver CTC program and count it among our military's best practices.[137] However, our leadership cannot rest on the laurels of the high levels of unit readiness and training that the CTCs helped generate. As the venue for our capstone readiness training events, our CTCs require continuous adaptation and upgrades to appropriately prepare our units for the myriad of projected FSO commitments. Orchestrating relevant professional NTC experiences has never been easy, but in our current fiscally austere situation, changes to the exercise objectives and scenarios will intensify the challenges. As an institution, the Army must prioritize its ability to deliver world-class training venues to BCTs and other enablers. To do so, the Army must build on what the NTC has already accomplished. Deliberate thoughtful choices, including seeking and implementing organic and other reduced cost opportunities to advance the COE's operational variable authenticity, should guide future investment of precious resources. Such synergistic efforts will ensure the NTC sustains graduating units with the optimal preparation for commitment in action. Beyond the individual units they touch, relevant and incremental adaptations at the NTC will strengthen the institutional role it plays towards propagating hard-won lessons and best practices across the JIIM community.[138]

Endnotes

[1] Barak Obama, "President's Speech at the U.S. Naval Academy on May 22, 2009," quoted in U.S. Department of the Army, The Army Capstone Concept, Operational Adaptability: Operating under Conditions of Uncertainty and Complexity in an Era of Persistent Conflict (2016-2028), Training and Doctrine Command Pamphlet (TRADOC Pam) 525-3-0 (Washington, DC: U.S. Department of the Army, December 21, 2009), 19-20.

[2] The U.S. Army maintains four Combat Training Centers (CTCs). The three oriented towards predominantly live maneuver training at the Brigade Combat Team-level (BCT) and below are: the National Training Center (NTC) at Fort Irwin, CA, the Joint Readiness Training Center (JRTC) at Fort Polk, LA, and the Joint Multinational Readiness Center (JMRC) at Hohenfels, Germany. The Army re-designated its fourth CTC, previously known as the Battle Command Training Program (BCTP), as the Mission Command Training Program (MCTP) in 2011. MCTP focuses on computer assisted staff training exercises for the brigade headquarters and above echelons. Since this paper focuses on the maneuver CTCs, specifically the NTC, the MCTP is not addressed in this paper. The U.S. Marine Corps also operates a maneuver CTC, the Air Ground Combat Center, located at Twentynine Palms, CA. U.S. Government, Accountability Office, Military Training – Army and Marine Corps Face Challenges to Address Projected Future Requirements: Report to Congressional Committees (Washington, DC: U.S. Government Accountability Office, July 2010), 6-7; James D. Crabtree, "Battle Command Training Program now Mission Command Training Program," May 12, 2011, linked from The United States Army Home Page at http://www.army.mil/article/56455/ (accessed February 18, 2012).

[3] Institute of Land Warfare, Association of the United States Army, Torchbearer National Security Report: U.S. Army Training for Unified Land Operations (Arlington, VA: Association of the United States Army, 2011), 8.

[4] Dennis Steele, "NTC: Between Hollywood and Hell," Army Magazine, July 2008, 34-36.

[5] According to Training Circular (TC) 7-101, Exercise Design, "the objective of exercise design is to structure a training event that establishes the conditions to facilitate performance-oriented training on properly selected, directed, and mission essential training objectives. U.S. Department of the Army, Exercise Design, Training and Doctrine Command Circular (TC) 7-101 (Washington, DC: U.S. Department of the Army, November 2010), vii.

[6] Institute of Land Warfare, Torchbearer National Security Report, 9.

[7] In this context, I describe "texture" as the bits of details and construction add-ons that contribute to making training more realistic. Examples include everything from role players, signs, rubbish, and knickknacks, to mosques. Steele, "NTC: Between Hollywood and Hell," 28; Associated, "atmospherics" are "the set dressings, to make you really think you are in that venue, the sights and smells and sounds....These include clothing dangling from a clothes line on a roof. Markets that include what looks like fresh beef, fish, and produce....even rubble piles that are calculated to portray what would happen if the building were hit by an explosive." Darrell R. Santschi, "Marines Unveil City-Size Urban Warfare Training At Twentynine Palms," The Press Enterprise, January 26, 2011, http://www.pe.com/local-news/san-bernardino-county/san-bernardino-county-headlines-index/20110127-marines-unveil-city-size-urban-warfare-training-at-twentynine-palms.ece (accessed December 13, 2011).

[8] U.S. Department of the Army, *The United States Army Operating Concept: 2016-2028*, Training and Doctrine Command Pamphlet (TRADOC Pam) 525-3-1 (Washington, DC: U.S. Department of the Army, August 19, 2010), 35.

[9] Institute of Land Warfare, *Torchbearer National Security Report,* 3.

[10] The U.S. Army defines the Contemporary Operational Environment (COE) as: The collective conditions, derived from a composite of actual worldwide conditions, that pose realistic challenges for training, leader development, and capabilities development for Army forces and their joint, intergovernmental, interagency and multinational partners. U.S. Department of the Army, *Exercise Design*, Glossary-4.

[11] John M. McHugh and Raymond T. Odierno, *A Statement on the Posture of the United States Army 2012,* Posture Statement presented to the 112th Cong., 2nd sess. (Washington, DC: U.S. Department of the Army, 2012), 5-6.

[12] Institute of Land Warfare, *Torchbearer National Security Report,* 4.

[13] U.S. Department of the Army, *The United States Army Operating Concept,* 11.

[14] Operational variables are: Political, Military, Economic, Social, Information, Infrastructure, Physical Environment, and Time (PMESII-PT). U.S. Department of the Army, *Exercise Design*, Glossary-4.

[15] U.S. Department of the Army, *Training Units and Developing Leaders for Full Spectrum Operations*, Army Field Manual (FM) 7-0 (Washington, DC: U.S. Department of the Army, February 2011), 14.

[16] Author's personal experience in units preparing for and participating in nine CTC rotations from 1991-1999.

[17] GlobalSecurity.org, "Fort Irwin," December 13, 2011, http://www.globalsecurity.org/military/facility/fort-irwin.htm (accessed December 13, 2011).

[18] The COE replicated at the JRTC was predominantly oriented at preparing brigade task forces for small-scale contingency (SSC) operations where the RTU would operate against a combination of primarily lightly-equipped conventional forces and their Irregular Warfare allies. To produce the appropriate battlefield and / or stability operations dynamics, JRTC increasingly moved to include rural and urban infrastructure inhabited by civilian on the battlefield (COB) role players. By 1996, JRTC had incorporated a major third world town (with 29 buildings), an airfield (with eight buildings), a mock military installation (with five buildings), as well multiple small villages and farms throughout the training area. The 14 training days of the former JRTC rotations typically consisted of two phases: an Irregular Warfare phase that emphasized operations under COIN conditions and then a MCO type of offensive and/or defensive fight phase. From the mid-1990s until 2003, JRTC and CMTC conducted episodic Mission Rehearsal Exercises (MREs) or Partnership-for-Peace (PFP) exercises instead of traditional rotations. These MREs were tailored to prepare designated U.S units for their upcoming Stability Operation deployments. PFP rotations included extensive foreign troops and employed Stability Operations themes; aiming to enhance military-to-military interoperability and build partner capacity. The U.S. engagement in Afghanistan and Iraq heightened JRTC's understanding and

focus on the importance of replicating adequate infrastructure and interaction with the population; areas where JRTC had proven successful, on a smaller scale, while training units for SSCs and Stabiliity Operations during the 1990s. By 2005, JRTC had increased its "box" infrastructure to contain about 11,000 buildings that comprised 18 towns and urban sprawl. Author's personal experience in units preparing for and participating in nine CTC rotations from 1991-1999; GlobalSecurity.org, "Fort Polk – Joint Readiness Training Center (JRTC)," http://www.globalsecurity.org/military/facility/fort-polk.htm (accessed March 20, 2012; Antony Joseph, "Training Today's Soldiers At JRTC: Joint Readiness Training Center," *Soldiers Magazine*, September 2005, linked from http://www.findarticles.com/p/articles/mi_m0OXU/is_9_60/ai_n15675505/ (accessed March 20, 2012).

[19] Gary W. Johnston, World-Class Army Adaptive Training: Next Steps, Strategy Research Project (Carlisle Barracks, PA: U.S. Army War College, March 13, 2009), 14.

[20] U.S. Government Accountability Office, *Military Training,* 4.

[21] Headquarters, National Training Center and Fort Irwin, "Conserve Resources to Sustain the NTC: The Army's Preeminent Landpower Tactical Lyceum", briefing slides, Fort Irwin, CA, July 12, 2011, http://www.smrconference.com/getfile.cfm?ID=73 (accessed 13 December 13, 2011).

[22] Headquarters, National Training Center and Fort Irwin, "Facts And Figures," http://www.irwin.army.mil/Visitors/INFO/Pages/FactsandFigures.aspx (accessed December 13, 2011).

[23] Some of the routine areas that NTC cadre and civilian subject matter experts (SMEs) work with the RTU at the individual, squad, and staff section-levels include: employing the latest command and control systems, non-lethal engagements, employing robotics, CREW, route clearance, counter-IED and sniper, biometrics, UAVs, advanced search techniques, and media engagements. Headquarters, National Training Center and Fort Irwin, "Transitioning NTC Rotations To Full Spectrum Operations," briefing slides used to brief the Chief of Staff of the Army, Fort Irwin, CA, August 14, 2008.

[24] U.S. Government Accountability Office, *Military Training,* 6.

[25] Martin E. Dempsey, "Front & Center: Training Development for an Expeditionary Army," *Army Magazine*, June 2009, 16.

[26] Steele, "NTC: Between Hollywood and Hell," 38.

[27] Author's personal experience as a Squadron Commander with the 11th Armored Cavalry Regiment (11th ACR) during 22 BCT rotations at the NTC from 2008-2010.

[28] Steele, "NTC: Between Hollywood and Hell," 38, 41.

[29] Headquarters, National Training Center and Fort Irwin, "Conserve Resources"

[30] Steele, "NTC: Between Hollywood and Hell," 28.

[31] Author's personal experience with the 11th ACR at the NTC from 2008-2010.

[32] NTC's National Urban Warfare Complex is part of one of the Box's two largest towns, Medina Jabal. This state-of-the-art urban combat training facility is used throughout each rotation, but is specifically designed for unit use in order to hone their skills, frequently with simunitions. There are networked cameras in each room and live-feed location updates on each Soldier assist the staff monitor unit performance. The complex also has shoot through the wall capabilities to more accurately assess weapon system effects. Charles Melton, "The National Training Center: NTC Uses Technology to Keep Soldiers Sharp Before Entering Combat Theaters," *Military Training Technology.com* 15, no. 1 (February 2010): 3 http://www.military-training-technology.com/mt2-home/227-mt2-2010-volume-15-issue-1/2531-command-profile-the-national-training-center.pdf (accessed December 13, 2011).

[33] U.S. Department of the Army, "Combat Training Center Program," information paper prepared by the HQDA G37/Collective Training Division for submission with Statement on the Posture of the United States Army 2011, Washington, DC, as of July 2011, https://secureweb2.hqda.pentagon.mil/VDAS_ArmyPostureStatement/2011/information_papers/PostedDocument.asp?id=264, (accessed December 13, 2011).

[34] Author's personal experience with the 11th ACR at the NTC from 2008-2010.

[35] The following example of background information, covering "General Role Player Motivation" for one character during a NTC Iraq focused MRE, represents a small portion of the background information each role player receives concerning the character he/she will portray: *Your father runs the construction company and has done very well with landing the company many jobs. With the new local government being established, there have been many opportunities to rebuild Medina Jabal. You have tried to get your father to build the new constructions with a look at integrity but he sees it more from the bottom line perspective, the more money the company makes, the better. You can foresee having to fix the buildings in the future due to the many short cuts that your father demands and you and your brothers do. Your mother is a nurse at the local hospital. You support the new government, but are very suspicious of the US Army and what they are really here for. You look to have the Allied Forces leave Iraq as soon as possible, though you have no ill will for the Americans. Your grandfather, Azim died in 1990 due to a heart attack and your grandmother, Amtullah, died in 1975 due to an untreated infection received from a scorpion bite on her lower leg.* U.S. Department of the Army, 11th Armored Cavalry Regiment, *Card 301E: Role Player Standards and Procedures*, (Fort Irwin, CA: 11th Armored Cavalry Regiment, January 10, 2009) References.

[36] Author's personal experience with the 11th ACR at the NTC from 2008-2010; Headquarters, NTC and Fort Irwin, "Transitioning NTC Rotations To FSO."

[37] Ibid.

[38] John M. McHugh and George W. Casey Jr., *A Statement on the Posture of the United States Army 2011*, Posture Statement presented to the 112th Cong., 1st sess. (Washington, DC: U.S. Department of the Army, 2011), 2.

[39] "Author Not Provided," "3rd ID Trains At NTC," *Fort Irwin (CA) High Desert Warrior*, March 15, 2012 linked from Headquarters, National Training Center and Fort Irwin, the "Community, Post Newspaper," http://www.irwin.army.mil/Pages/default.aspx (accessed March 19, 2012).

[40] U.S. Department of the Army, *The United States Army Operating Concept,* 6-7.

[41] U.S. Department of the Army, *The Army Capstone Concept,* 9; Johnston, "World-Class Army Adaptive Training: Next Steps," 2.

[42] Andrew Tilghman, "DoD Wants To Shed Troops As Fast As Possible," *Army Times,* February 27, 2012.

[43] Richard H. Sinnreich, "Maybe It's Time To Channel George F. Kennan," *Army Magazine,* February 2012, 20.

[44] Chris Budihas, "The Strategic Importance of U.S. Forces in Europe," *Army Magazine,* February 2012, 21.

[45] Sinnreich, "Maybe It's Time," 20.

[46] Budihas, "The Strategic Importance," 21.

[47] Sinnreich, "Maybe It's Time," 20; Budihas, "The Strategic Importance," 21.

[48] Nathan Freier et al., *U.S. Ground Force Capabilities through 2020,* (Washington, DC: Center For Strategic & International Studies, 2011), ix.

[49] McHugh and Casey, *U.S. Army Posture Statement 2011,* 15.

[50] John A. Nagl, "Let's Win the Wars We're In," *Joint Force Quarterly* 52 (1st quarter 2009): 25.

[51] Jim Garamone, "Obama: Defense Strategy Will Maintain U.S. Military Pre-eminence," *American Forces Press Service,* January 5, 2012, http://www.defense.gov/news/newsarticle.aspx?id=66683 (accessed January 6, 2012).

[52] U.S. Department of Defense, *Sustaining U.S. Global Leadership: Priorities for 21st Century Defense,* (Washington, DC: U.S. Department of Defense, January 2012), 7-8.

[53] David E. Johnson et al, *Preparing And Training For The Full Spectrum Of Military Challenges: Insights From The Experiences Of China, France, The United Kingdom, India And Israel* (Santa Monica, CA: RAND Corporation, 2009), 256.

[54] Robert H. Scales Robert H. Scales, "The 7,000: What history tells us we'll need tomorrow," *Armed Forces Journal* 149, no. 5 (December 2011): 24.

[55] Richard Weitz, "Global Insights: Righting Trans-Atlantic Defense Spending in 2012," *World Politics Review Online,* (January 3, 2012): 1. http://www.scribd.com/doc/77042021/Global-Insights-Righting-Trans-Atlantic-Defense-Spending-in-2012 (accessed 3 January 3, 2012).

[56] Johnson, *Preparing And Training For The Full Spectrum,* 228; Andrew F. Krepinevich, *Strategy for the Long Haul: An Army at the Crossroads,* Center for Strategic and Budgetary

Assessments series on defense issues (Washington, DC: Center for Strategic and Budgetary Assessments, 2008), 2-3.

[57] Strategy Page, "The Contemporary Operational Environment (COE)," December 8, 2011, http://www.strategypage.com/articles/operationenduringfreedom/chap1.asp (accessed December 8, 2011).

[58] Ibid.

[59] U.S. Department of the Army, *Training Units and Developing Leaders,* 1-2.

[60] Dempsey, "Front & Center: Training Development," 14; William Fleser, "Preparing For Hybrid Threats: Improving Force Preparation for Irregular Warfare," *Special Warfare Magazine*, May-June 2010, 10.

[61] Strategy Page, "The Contemporary Operational Environment (COE)"

[62] U.S. Department of the Army, *The United States Army Operating Concept,* 9; Robert M. Gates, "Speech by then-Secretary of Defense Robert M. Gates at West Point, NY," February 25, 2011, http://www.defense.gov/speeche/speech.asx?speechid=1539, (accessed December 13, 2011).

[63] U.S. Department of the Army, *The Army Capstone Concept,* 11, 62.

[64] Johnston, "World-Class Army Adaptive Training: Next Steps," 3.

[65] Krepinevich, *Strategy for the Long Haul,* 3.

[66] Institute of Land Warfare, Torchbearer National Security Report, 16; Scott Efflandt, "Unit of Action: Organizing the Brigade Combat Team for Future Wars," *Military Review* 90, no. 4 (July-August 2010): 28.

[67] Fleser, "Preparing For Hybrid Threats," 11; Johnson, *Preparing And Training For The Full Spectrum,* 228.

[68] Nagl, "Let's Win the Wars We're In," 25; U.S. Department of the Army, *The United States Army Operating Concept,* 9.

[69] Krepinevich, *Strategy for the Long Haul,* 11.

[70] Fleser, "Preparing For Hybrid Threats," 11.

[71] U.S. Department of the Army, *Training Units and Developing Leaders,* 1-1.

[72] Gates, "Speech at West Point, NY."

[73] Freier, *U.S. Ground Force Capabilities through 2020,* 4.

[74] Sinnreich, "Maybe It's Time," 20.

[75] Gates, "Speech at West Point, NY"; Strategy Page, "The Contemporary Operational Environment (COE)"; McHugh and Casey, *U.S. Army Posture Statement 2011,* 11.

[76] Freier, *U.S. Ground Force Capabilities through 2020,* 4.

[77] U.S. Department of Defense, *Sustaining U.S. Global Leadership,* President's Memorandum, SECDEF Memorandum, 1, 3, 6.

[78] Robert Killebrew, "Cutbacks and Crisis: How the military must adapt to an era of shrinking budgets and growing threats," *Armed Forces Journal* 149, no. 5 (December 2011): 149, no. 5 (December 2011): 18.

[79] U.S. Department of the Army, *The Army Capstone Concept,* i.

[80] U.S. Department of the Army, *The United States Army Operating Concept,* 6-7.

[81] U.S. Department of the Army, *Operations,* Field Manual 3.0 (Washington, DC: U.S. Department of the Army, February 27, 2008), 3-6, quoted in Krepinevich, *Strategy for the Long Haul,* 47.

[82] Institute of Land Warfare, *Torchbearer National Security Report,* 3.

[83] Lance M. Bacon, "Army To Lose Another 5 BCTs: Total Will Drop To 32, Chief of Staff Says," *Army Times,* March 5, 2012.

[84] Johnson, *Preparing And Training For The Full Spectrum,* 232.

[85] Freier, *U.S. Ground Force Capabilities through 2020,* 16-17.

[86] Ibid., vii; Krepinevich, *Strategy for the Long Haul,* 62.

[87] Johnson, *Preparing And Training For The Full Spectrum,* 234.

[88] Krepinevich, *Strategy for the Long Haul,* 31.

[89] Gian P. Gentile, "Let's Build an Army to Win All Wars," *Joint Force Quarterly* 52 (1st quarter 2009): 33.

[90] Freier, *U.S. Ground Force Capabilities through 2020,* 4; U.S. Department of the Army, *The United States Army Operating Concept,* 6-7.

[91] Krepinevich, *Strategy for the Long Haul,* 50.

[92] Freier, *U.S. Ground Force Capabilities through 2020,* vii; Gentile, "Let's Build an Army to Win All Wars," 33.

[93] Freier, *U.S. Ground Force Capabilities through 2020,* vi-vii, 16.

[94] Ibid., 9, 16.

[95] Nagl, "Let's Win the Wars We're In," 25.

[96] Gentile, "Let's Build an Army to Win All Wars," 31.

[97] Ibid., 32.

[98] Krepinevich, *Strategy for the Long Haul,* 64.

[99] Jon Oltsik, "Russian Cyber Attack on Georgia: Lessons Learned?" *Network World*, August 17, 2009, http:www.networkworld.com/community/node/44448, quoted in The Small Wars Journal, "Cyberwar Case Study: Georgia 2008," January 6, 2011, http://smallwarsjournal.com/blog/journal/docs-temp/639-hollis.pdf (accessed March 6, 2012).

[100] Freier, *U.S. Ground Force Capabilities through 2020,* vii.

[101] Johnson, *Preparing And Training For The Full Spectrum,* 231; Fleser, "Preparing For Hybrid Threats," 11-12; Gentile, "Let's Build an Army to Win All Wars," 31.

[102] Efflandt, "Unit of Action," 28.

[103] U.S. Department of the Army, *Training Units and Developing Leaders,* 2-3.

[104] Johnson, *Preparing And Training For The Full Spectrum,* xx.

[105] Ibid., 232.

[106] U.S. Department of Defense, *Sustaining U.S. Global Leadership,* 1.

[107] U.S. Department of the Army, *The Army Capstone Concept,* 9.

[108] Gentile, "Let's Build an Army to Win All Wars," 28.

[109] Department of the Army, Department of the Army, "Full Spectrum Training Concept," information paper prepared by the HQDA G37/Collective Training Division for submission with Statement on the Posture of the United States Army 2011, Washington, DC, as of July 2011, https://secureweb2.hqda.pentagon.mil/VDAS_ArmyPostureStatement/2011/information_papers/PostedDocument.asp?id=270 , (accessed December 13, 2011); Dempsey, "Front & Center: Training Development," 14.

[110] U.S. Department of the Army, *Training Units and Developing Leaders,* 1-2.

[111] U.S. Department of the Army, *The Army Capstone Concept,* 8.

[112] Krepinevich, *Strategy for the Long Haul,* xii; Freier, *U.S. Ground Force Capabilities through 2020*, 9.

[113] Bacon, "Army To Lose Another 5 BCTs"

[114] U.S Joint Chiefs of Staff, *America's Military – A Profession Of Arms: White Paper,* (Washington, DC: U.S. Joint Chiefs of Staff, February 23, 2012), 6, http://www.cannon.af.mil/shared/media/document/AFD-120229-062.pdf (accessed March 7, 2012) quoted in "Author Not Provided," "The Military: We Must Be Proficient In More Than Combat," *Army Times,* March 12, 2002.

115 Dempsey, "Front & Center: Training Development," 14.

116 U.S. Department of the Army, *The Army Capstone Concept,* 7.

117 Johnson, *Preparing And Training For The Full Spectrum,* xx.

118 Denver Makle, "U.S. Army in Europe shifts from COIN to full-spectrum training," October 5, 2011, linked from U.S. Army Europe Home Page, http://www.eur.army.mil/news/archive2011/10052011-fste.htm (accessed November 22, 2011).

119 Strategy Page, "The Contemporary Operational Environment (COE)"

120 U.S. Department of the Army, *Training Units and Developing Leaders,* 1-2; U.S. Department of the Army, *The Army Capstone Concept,* 27.

121 U.S. Department of the Army, *The United States Army Operating Concept,* 6.

122 Krepinevich, *Strategy for the Long Haul,* 22-23.

123 Strategy Page, "The Contemporary Operational Environment (COE)"; TC 7-101 indicates that available exercise resources, to include training areas, support, and simulation, are some of the key considerations that the exercise director and planners incorporate into exercise design. U.S. Department of the Army, *Exercise Design*, 2-2.

124 Ibid., Glossary 4.

125 Frank Oliveri, "The Army Reloads Its Training Strategy," *CQ Weekly* (August 16, 2010): 1966. http://library.cqpress.com/cqweekly/weeklyreport111-000003722770 (accessed December 2, 2011).

126 The NTC was successful in previous projects on main post. Author's personal experience with the 11th ACR at the NTC from 2008-2010.

127 Author's personal experience with the 11th ACR at the NTC from 2008-2010.

128 Headquarters, NTC and Fort Irwin, "Facts And Figures."

129 U.S. Department of the Army, *Exercise Design*, 3-12.

130 Author's personal experience with the 11th ACR at the NTC from 2008-2010.

131 U.S. Department of the Army, *Exercise Design*, 3-12.

132 Ibid.

133 Steele, "NTC: Between Hollywood and Hell," 32.

134 Ibid., 45.

135 McHugh and Odierno, *U.S. Army Posture Statement 2012,* 5-6.

[136] Steele, "NTC: Between Hollywood and Hell," 46, 48.

[137] Johnson, *Preparing And Training For The Full Spectrum,* 234.

[138] Institute of Land Warfare, *Torchbearer National Security Report,* 2.